WRITING PROMPTS for THRILLER WRITERS

Sharpen your writing technique with #1 bestselling thriller author

JANE HOLLAND

Copyright @ Jane Holland 2019

All rights reserved.

Published by Thimblerig Books

The moral right of the author has been asserted.

No part of this book can be reproduced or transferred by any means without the express written permission of the author.

ISBN: 9781089398097

How to use this book

This is a book for writers by a professional writer, someone who knows what it's like to get up in the morning and stare at a blank sheet of paper.

Regardless of where you are in your writing career – just starting out, published a few, bestseller, returning after a break – we're all *writers*, and we all know the perennial obstacles to writing.

One key obstacle is fear: fear of failure, fear of success, fear of looking stupid, fear of just about anything. Another is creative apathy. Then there's mental fatigue. Lack of inspiration. Uncertainty about your own strengths and limitations. Maybe you just aren't sure what you want to write. Or you can't believe anyone will want to read what you've written.

This is a workbook of detailed writing prompts for those moments. But it also contains useful thoughts on writing fiction, word sprint exercises, lists of thrillerish words, and pages for notes and rough drafts.

Use the prompts to inspire your writing. Start a rough draft here, if you wish, and continue onscreen or in a notebook. Good luck!

Jane Holland

"PRO WRITERS keep their hand in by writing little and often.

Never let even the busiest day go by without laying a few words of your novel down …"

WRITING PROMPT

It's night and you're hiding in a priest's house, which is being searched.

Who's hunting you and why are you in danger?

Who is the priest and why is he shielding you? Where exactly are you hiding?

What will happen if you're found? Both to the priest and to you?

Concentrate on hearing and touch. These two senses, in particular, bring a story alive.

WRITING PROMPT

Write a short scene in which the colour or scent of lilacs is central to the story.

Incorporate three or more of the following elements:

A monkey puzzle tree

Clogs

A tarot card

A key

The sound of a gunshot

Snakeskin

NOTES

"PLOTTER OR PANTSER, you need to keep the shape of the book in your head as you write.

That's best done by writing in a linear fashion, not out of sequence, and regularly touching base with your novel."

WRITING PROMPT

You wake up to find you've been buried alive …

What do you do first?

How does your body react?

What can you see? What can you smell, hear, feel? Do you say anything? Shout or scream? Are you gagged?

Who put you there and why? Do you know?

Write this scene as quickly as possible.

NOTES

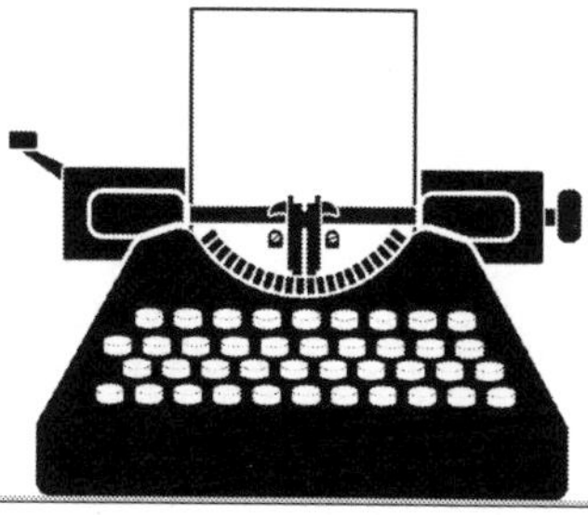

WRITING PROMPT

A woman finds a clothed dead body on the beach.

Before calling the police, she searches the dead body and removes an item.

She doesn't mention this to the police.

Later she makes another phone call.

Is she alone when she finds the body? Who is the deceased? Does she know him/her? To whom does she make the call, and why?

Show her physical reactions rather than telling us her emotional state.

Do not explain what she took from the body, or why she took it, until the last line.

You can choose not to reveal the whole truth. But, as the author, you should know, and make it possible for a good reader to guess.

WRITING PROMPT

Write a scene in which someone is having their leg sawn off.

Choose one of two points-of-view.

Either the person whose leg is being sawn off, or the person doing the sawing.

Include these words:

Petal
Diamond
Exquisite
Backfire
Rollercoaster

NOTES

WRITING PROMPT

You are a ten-year-old watching a man abducting your mother.

You know the man.

Who is he? What is his connection with your family?

Where are you, and why?

What gender are you? What are you wearing? What is your mother wearing? What time of day or night is it?

Why do you remain silent?

Incorporate these words:
'Behind the eyes, nothing …'

NOTES

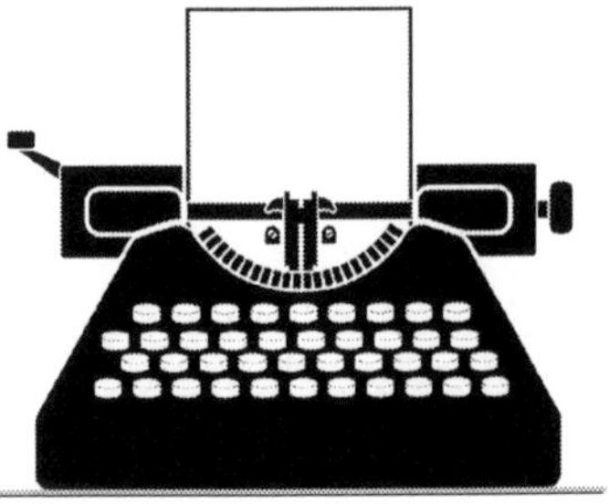

WORD SPRINTS

Sit down and write for 10 minutes. Write a detailed character study of a stranger walking past or sitting nearby, or whom you saw recently. Give them a secret. Then relax!

WRITING PROMPT

A woman is lying in a sunlit field, listening to a bird singing just out of sight.

She is dying, and she knows it.

Before she dies, she wants to leave a message behind for those who eventually find her.

Who is she? What happened and why?

What is the message or clue she is so desperate to leave behind? Describe in elaborate detail how she contrives this.

Describe her last moments. Her physical and emotional state. Who or what is she thinking about?

Use repetition as an effect.

NOTES

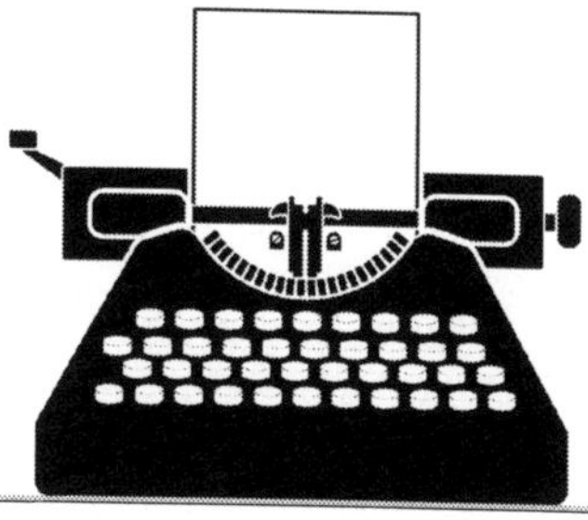

WRITING PROMPT

You have killed someone but not admitted it, and have concealed the body.

Perhaps it was an accident, and you're in agonies over it. But perhaps it was deliberate and you're ecstatic.

Write a short scene where you discuss the deceased – who only appears to be missing at this point – while trying to conceal what you've done from someone who knows you well, i.e. a parent, adult sibling or spouse.

The body is nearby. Where?

You have to trick or persuade your loved one away from the dead body's hiding place.

Keep dialogue short and telling, with lots of clever subtext to increase tension. Employ dramatic irony – that's where the reader knows more than the characters.

NOTES

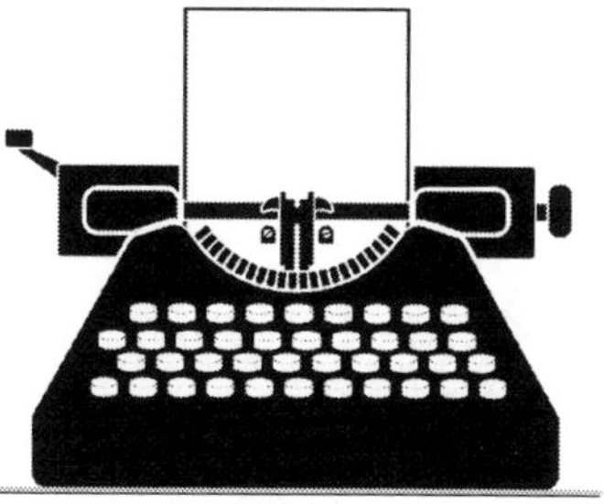

WORD SPRINTS

Wherever you are, stop and write for 10 minutes. Describe a sinister weather experience, from the point of view of someone in danger, hiding out. Then relax!

"WHO, WHEN, WHERE, WHAT, WHY?

There's no shame in planning, and much reward.

If an inexperienced writer can't or won't answer the five W's before writing their first line, odds are high they'll fall by the wayside without ever reaching their last one."

WRITING PROMPT

'Hell hath no fury as a woman scorned!'

Write a short scene in which a woman has been scorned and is doing something hellish about it.

Use dialogue to suggest anger, but without explaining backstory.

This is a key technique in writing a page-turner.

It forces the reader to develop theories and ask questions that will remain unanswered, at least until the next question is raised.

They will keep reading to discover the truth … and test their theories, of course!

NOTES

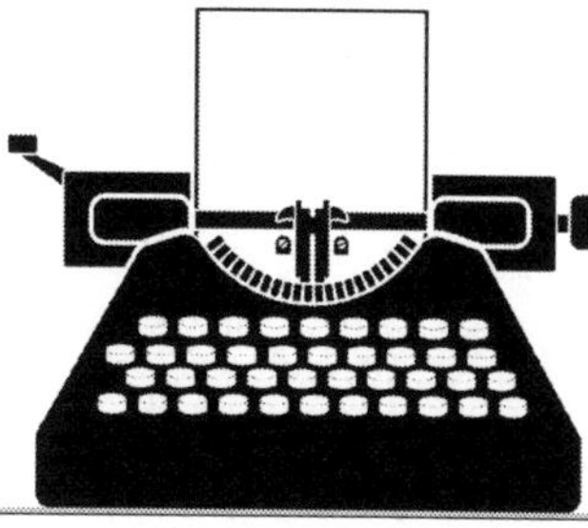

"FIRST PAGES – These should encapsulate the central premise of the book, or at least suggest what lies ahead."

WRITING PROMPT

A police officer has to break into a house where the occupant hasn't been seen for some days.

The officer is alone and can't wait for back-up. Why not?

Describe the interior of the house with close attention. It should be old, dirty, smelly, unloved.

Think about size, dimensions, realism. Be visual. Use the senses. Let each 'telling detail' paint a picture for us.

There are strange noises from behind one closed door.

The officer is apprehensive, but opens the door and discovers … what?

Choose either a grim find, or an unexpected one.

NOTES

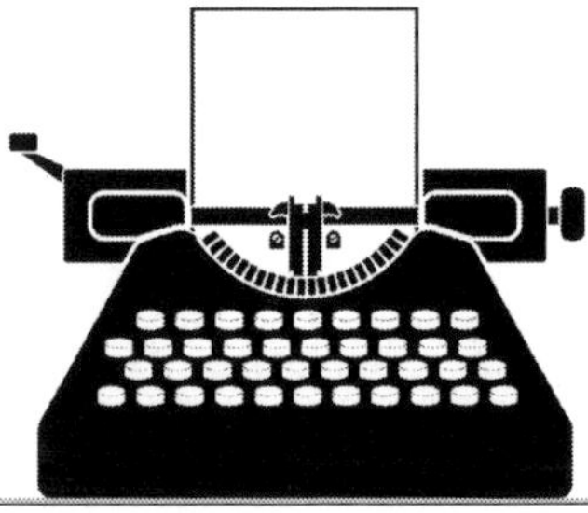

WRITING PROMPT

Describe waking up in a car wreck.

You're disorientated and injured, you can't remember what happened or where you were going.

But you know your newborn was in a car seat in the back. You turn to check she's okay … But she's gone!

Panicked, you hunt for your mobile phone to call the police.

But there's a text on your phone that stops you in your tracks.

What does it say? Is it a warning or an instruction? What do you do next?

Use the colour blue repeatedly, in different forms, and layer in metaphors for spirituality. Unexpected touches like this can deepen a text.

NOTES

WORD SPRINTS

These are perfect for day job writers. Grab 10 mins at lunch or on the commute. Write the diary entry of a deranged individual planning a murder. Then relax!

"CHARACTERS come to life when other characters talk about them.

A character in isolation is much harder to draw than one with friends, loved ones, colleagues – and particularly enemies."

WRITING PROMPT

Describe the routine of a trained assassin as they prepare to kill a target.

Is the assassin male or female?

What do they do to prepare? Think about weapons, timing, phone calls, clothing, route, hiding places.

What kind of feelings do they experience?

Is it a ritual or is every time different?

Describe the moment of the kill. Consider the senses in minute detail.

What are the first 3 things the assassin does immediately afterwards?

NOTES

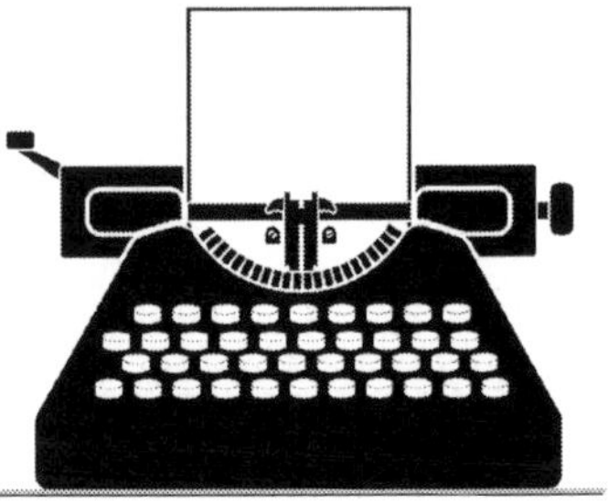

WRITING PROMPT

Use a nursery rhyme – search online if one doesn't readily spring to mind – as the basis for a grim scene or storyline.

If you chose 'Polly put the kettle on,' for instance, you might set a scene in a kitchen.

Have a character called Polly making refreshments. Is she happy or resentful? Is she alone or is there someone with her? Who's she making tea for, and why?

Now introduce a sinister note.

Is that an undetectable poison Polly's slipping into the teapot? Is she planning to murder someone with that bread knife, etc?

Avoid any descent into comedy or parody, unless you actively want that. Keep the line taut.

NOTES

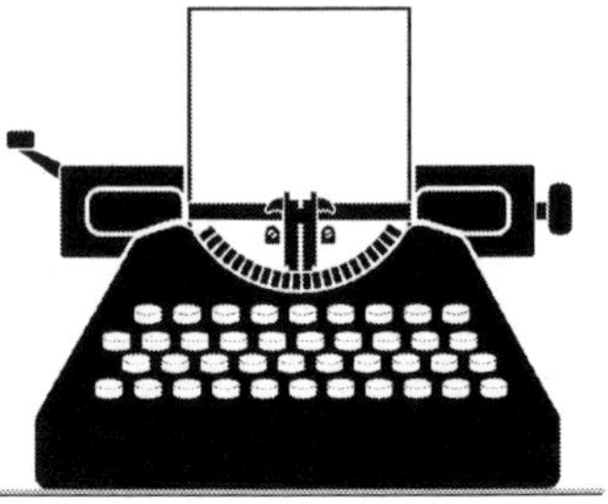

"DON'T LISTEN to so-called experts who tell you what to write and what not to write, or dismiss your novel as unpublishable.

In this industry, nobody knows what will sell and what won't. They just don't want you to suspect that sad truth."

WRITING PROMPT

Write a short story under 3000 words with the title, RED HOLIDAY.

Include these elements:

Faded petals

A popular song from the past or classical music

Something buried

The number 9

NOTES

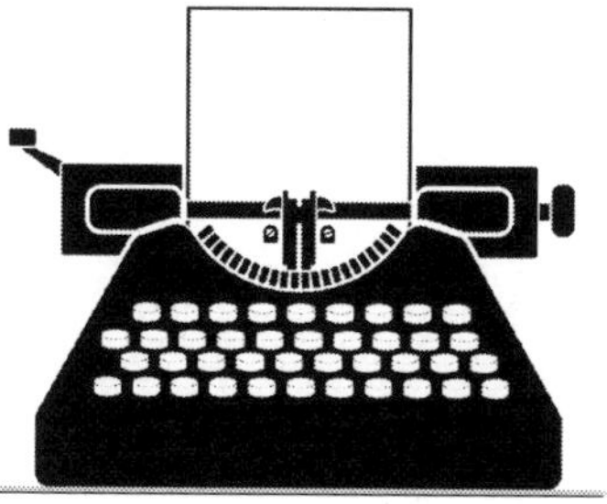

WRITING PROMPT

Take a walk in the skin of one of your own ancestors.

Choose or create a long-dead relative, preferably someone who died before you were born.

In their point-of-view, imagine your relative about to commit a crime.

They're afraid, but only in case they get caught.

What is the crime, and why are they even considering it?

Do they go through with it?

Work on developing empathy with your character – do this by becoming alert to how they inhabit the page in a physical sense, their gestures, their sensations, their voice, even their scent …

NOTES

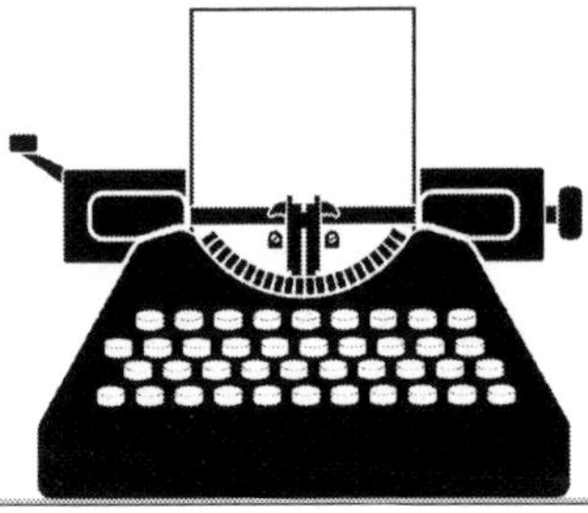

WORD SPRINTS

Take 10 minutes to work on characterisation in your current manuscript. Thrillers may be plot-heavy, but people drive the plots. Never let them act 'out of character'. Then relax!

"WRITING IS INTERIOR, publishing is exterior.

Try not to muddle the two up, and don't listen to those who think you can cross the streams with impunity!"

WRITING PROMPT

Two people get into a fight. One has a knife.

Describe the fight.

Where does it take place? Who are these two, and what is the confrontation about?

What kind of knife is it?

Fight scenes are among the hardest to write, partly because it's tempting to 'overdescribe' physical moves.

This can make fight scenes read clumsily.

Focus on lightly described choreography and the tension between assailants.

NOTES

WRITING PROMPT

The police come to your door on a hot day.

They're asking about a murder committed nearby, a door-to-door inquiry. You answer questions calmly and politely.

Meanwhile, in another room, the killer is holding your child hostage at knife-point.

Write this scene.

Focus on the police officers. Do you manage to subtly convey a message that something is wrong?

End with you returning to the killer and finding him gone – with your child.

NOTES

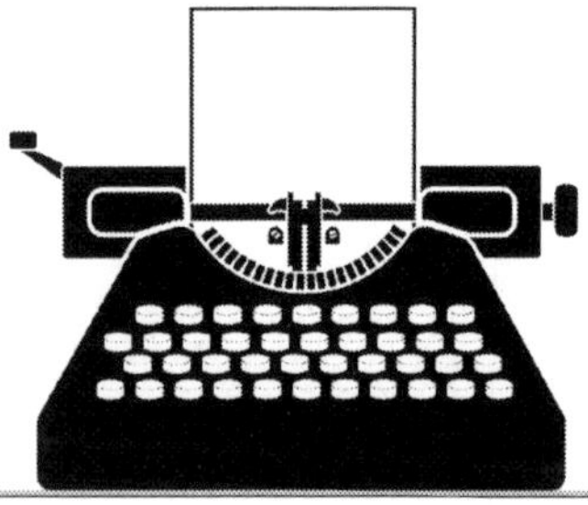

"SOME WRITERS SWEAR by character biographies.

They religiously note down what their characters eat for breakfast, the name of their first pet, how they loved green jelly as a child and used to race the bus on their bike.

I've never written a character biography.

I've spent fifty years watching people, I know them inside-out, and my characters are people. What they used to do when they were nine is immaterial, unless it impacts on the plot."

WRITING PROMPT

A loved one tells you they killed someone in the past.

You wrestle with the need to tell someone else – the police?

But you decide to keep it to yourself, telling yourself they've changed, and there were mitigating circumstances.

Until you fear they've done it again. And you may be next.

Write the scene where you realise this, while discussing something completely different with them.

Concentrate on dialogue and visuals.

NOTES

WRITING PROMPT

A woman is going door-to-door for a charity.

At one house, she hears a woman crying out. The man at the door is distracted and impatient, with deep red gouges across his face. He claims a cat scratched him.

He invites her in while he fetches his wallet. She goes in reluctantly, just to reassure herself no one is hurt.

What happens next? Choose one of these characters and write the scene from their POV.

Try to use as many proper nouns (names) as you can, i.e. Jane, Lycra, Canada. These add depth and a sense of verisimilitude to your world.

NOTES

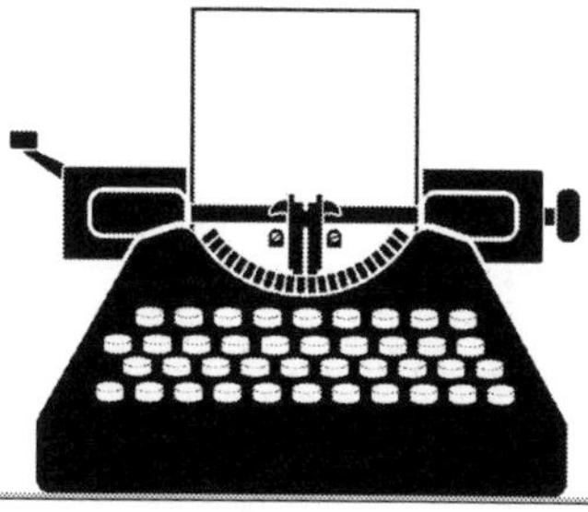

"SOME PEOPLE write fast. Others write slowly.

But like the hare and the tortoise, we all get there in the end ... unless we're foolish enough to give up.

So don't give up."

WORD SPRINTS

Take a load off, let your coffee cool, and write for 10 minutes. Write dialogue for two police officers discovering a body on waste ground. It's the spouse of one of the officers. OMG. Then relax!

NOTES

"DESPAIR can hollow out a writer.

The despair of rejection, the despair of publisher neglect, the despair of low sales, the despair of envy at other writers' successes, the despair of burn-out and creative apathy …

But give the same writer a whiff of a great story, and they start hammering the keys again with the excitement of a newbie.

Writing is in the blood, like an incurable disease. We write because that's who we are, that's what we do. Next time you fall into despair, remember that – and keep writing."

WRITING PROMPT

A veteran police officer, close to retirement, finds themselves unexpectedly in a life-and-death situation.

They've promised their family not to do anything dangerous in the last week at work. Yet here they are, risking their life.

Write this scene, incorporating 2 of these elements:

A Michael Jackson song

A mountain bike

Traffic lights

A photograph from WWII

A strong smell

NOTES

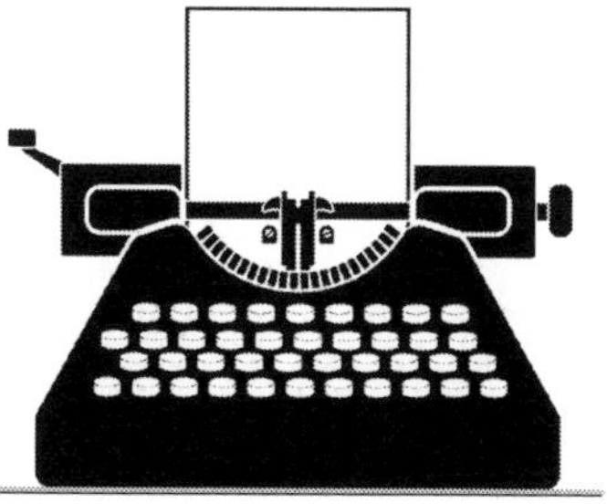

"WHEN YOU LOOK hard enough, everything is a metaphor for writing."

WRITING PROMPT

A man comes back early from work one day to find a strange car on his driveway.

He sneaks in the back of the house, and overhears a conversation between his wife and a strange man.

They are planning a murder. But not his, he gradually realises.

Who are they planning to murder – and why?

Write this three-hander, concentrating on a dialogue exchange between the couple that reveals clues very slowly, in a drip-feed way rather than all at once, to the silent shock of the man listening …

NOTES

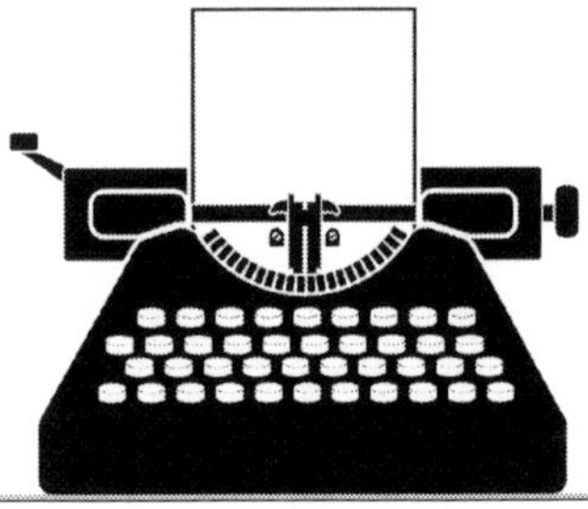

"WRITING is mathematical at heart. It's about weight, balance, shape, symmetry, numbers, adding, subtracting …

Read back what you've written. Listen for the rhythms, the ebb and flow, the emphases, the important pauses.

Invariably, a sentence will tell you where it's been calculated wrongly."

WRITING PROMPT

A woman in her fifties is fascinated by a young waitress in a café.

As they chat, the woman becomes more and more convinced that the younger woman is in fact her long-lost daughter, abducted as a five-year-old.

What does she do? How does she feel?

Then the waitress talks about her own parents … clearly believing them to be her own flesh and blood.

Write this scene, deciding in advance if the customer really is her mother.

NOTES

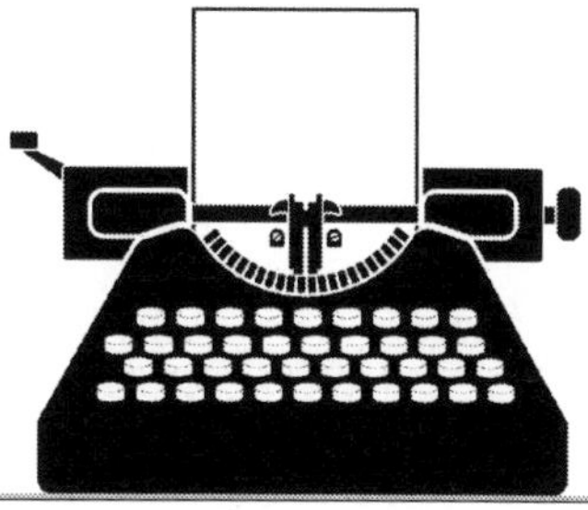

"IF YOU LOVE WRITING, and wish on it often enough, it will take you through the back of the wardrobe into a magical land of your own choosing.

That's what writing does for you. It's an escape. But it's also a responsibility.

Because once you've found that secret route, it's your sacred duty to come back and take others with you."

WRITING PROMPT

A budding novelist meets his favourite thriller writer at a festival.

After the book signing, he tells the famous author about a book with a stunningly unique plot that he's written. As the author listens, he realises the plot is exactly the same as the book he's nearly finished writing.

He knows if this wannabe approaches any of the agents at the festival with this 'unique' story, his own book could be dead in the water. And he has a huge tax bill.

They're alone together in a marquee after everyone else has left. There's a cake knife on the table …

Write this scene. What happens next?

NOTES

"IF REWARDS AND PUNISHMENTS don't get you writing, try coming at it from another angle …

Dictate your story using software like Dragon or record your voice and type it up later. Write longhand instead of straight to screen. Ask a friend or other half for a starting line, rather than relying on your own brain.

Keep one place strictly for writing, even if it's just a corner of your bedroom. Do anything, everything, whatever it takes, to start and keep writing.

Your mind doesn't like hard work. So you need to trick it. Once you're going, things should feel easier. Oil the squeaky hinge of your writing mind, and get it moving!"

WORD SPRINTS

Take 10 minutes to work on your current manuscript. Don't worry too much about what you write, just free-associate and let the words flow. Then relax!

"THINK OF WRITING as magic, and you as the magician.

Some days, the trick goes wrong. Other times, you pull it out of the hat and the crowd applauds!

Practice makes the latter happen more frequently than the former."

NOTES

NOTES

THRILLER WORD LIST

Keep these randomly compiled lists handy when writing your thriller or suspense novel, to aid in inspiration and word choice

soft-hued	stitch-up
fear	quiescent
target	past
rope	inimical
loveless	trapdoor
rotten	swindle
stifle	feigned
condemn	blood
miasma	observation
massacre	revenge
sacrifice	candlelight
suicide	hypocrisy
abattoir	gloaming
pallbearer	fragmentary
hic jacet	rancid
crime passionnel	disintegrate
bones	scaffold
stench	unsettle

evasion
trap
heinous
evil
extinction
forgotten
buried
deadly
hoodwink
bait
Machiavellian
sly
fraud
darkness
euthanasia
rigor mortis
inhuman
casket
lethal
garrotte
carnage
cull
embalm
skeletal
blear
hoax
plausible

poleaxe
carrion
zombie
exanimate
underworld
decapitate
ritual
crash
premeditated
electrocute
unknown
decompose
embers
occultation
lump
torso
shadowy
disintegrate
holy water
weapon
skulduggery
nebulous
snare
cadaverous
feigned
mildewed
vice

immolation
knell
cry havoc!
shroud
matricide
purge
fusillade
smite
crepuscular
corruption
rainy
charnel house
malignant
carcass
dust
Stygian
deadfall
ruse
footsteps
vulnerable
bad seed
innocence
veil
toxicology
obsequies
crypt

demise
mortuary
death row
loss
owl-light
conceal
dissect
liquefaction
dungeon
scrap
remorseless
trunk
nocturnal
raven
crudely
befogged
lantern
garbled
briny
silhouette
negative
moonless
bloodletting
fallen
lost
eternal

sarcophagus
hanged
smother
wall up
cutthroat
remains
detect
gaslight
ashes
tenebrous
worms
imperfect
decay
haziness
pitch
darkling
entropy
lake
deranged
absent
lurk
blackout
rot
slaughter
rites
necropolis

bloodbath
suttee
annihilate
departed
eclipse
cavern
quench
darkling
lynch
pistol
crucifixion
glimmer
umbra
moulder
earthlight
rags & tatters
dirge
opaque
sully
misadventure
carrion
goner
cortege
blight
poison
grave

deception	foul play
harmful	dusk
corpse	delapidated
malevolent	sooty
danger	drenched
witching time	parcel or plot
empty	meagre
detritus	slippery
dismember	trickster
tears	strangle
putrid	prevaricate
secrets	exsanguinate
sundown	scatter
wisp	morgue
snuff out	posthumous
stream	ossuary
chiaroscuro	sabre
chop	stiff
sombre	behead
dying	mourning
noose	coffin
chicanery	mummify
ambush	tripwire

"THE FIRST LINE is an invitation to the reader, to enter the magical territory of the story.

So try to make it sound like your novel is worth the journey."

Thank you for purchasing this 'Writing Prompts' workbook by Jane Holland

Discover Jane Holland's bestselling thrillers on Amazon.

All are available as ebooks via Kindle Unlimited or for paid download, and most are also in paperback.

GIRL NUMBER ONE
LOCK THE DOOR
FORGET HER NAME
ALL YOUR SECRETS
WHY SHE RAN
LAST BIRD SINGING
DEAD SIS
THE HIVE

Printed in Great Britain
by Amazon